THE LITTLE BOOK OF
SLEEP

PAUL WILSON

PENGUIN BOOKS

PENGUIN BOOKS

Published by the Penguin Group
Penguin Books Ltd, 27 Wrights Lane, London w8 5TZ, England
Penguin Putnam Inc., 375 Hudson Street, New York, New York 10014, USA
Penguin Books Australia Ltd, Ringwood, Victoria, Australia
Penguin Books Canada Ltd, 10 Alcorn Avenue, Toronto, Ontario, Canada M4V 3B2
Penguin Books (NZ) Ltd, Private Bag 102902 NSMC, Auckland, New Zealand

Penguin Books Ltd, Registered Offices: Harmondsworth, Middlesex, England

First published by Penguin Books Australia Ltd 1999
Published in Penguin Books 1999
1 3 5 7 9 10 8 6 4 2

Printed in England by William Clowes Ltd

Remember how wonderful it felt to awaken – refreshed, alive, eager to make the most of the day? With no recollection of the preceding eight hours except that it was deep, satisfying, undisturbed slumber?
Every morning could be like that.

Remember how your dreams could excite you, even days after the event? And those all-too-rare moments of bliss as you drifted off to sleep, your consciousness floating between illumination and tranquillity?
You can recapture those feelings tonight.

The Little Book of Sleep was created to add beauty to your slumber and make bedtime one of the highlights of your day.

Let this book fall open to any page for the suggestion that will work best for you tonight. Accept it at face value. Let your subconscious have its way. Then, lie back and enjoy it.

Oh, yes . . . and pleasant dreams!

Conquer all workplace tensions with
Paul Wilson's complete work,
Calm at Work.

TAKE REST

Take rest; a field that has rested gives a beautiful crop.

OVID

No time for the nightcap

There is a widespread belief that the sedating properties of alcohol will assist your sleep. Not so. In fact, the opposite is usually the case. While alcohol may sometimes invite sleep, it often disrupts the rest of your night by also inviting restlessness and early morning awakening.

PEACE COMES THROUGH THE WINDOW

Fresh air is one of the cheapest aids to a deep, satisfying rest. The more oxygen you imbibe, the more physically relaxed you will feel.

Leave the window open a little, even in cool weather, and allow sleep to breeze in in the most wholesome way.

COVER YOURSELF

As a baby you were conditioned to
believe that sound sleep and cosy
bedcovers went together.

You can take advantage of that
conditioning and recapture that
childlike sense of security by always
using a light cover when you sleep.
Even in warm weather, it works.

GIVE THANKS TO COWS

Old wives have been telling us this
since Adam was a baby, but milk really
does work as a soothing late night
drink. Because it contains calcium and
the amino acid tryptophan – both of
which help the body to relax – milk is
a natural aid to sleep.

MAKE YOUR COFFEE EARLY

Coffee and, to a lesser extent, tea were purpose designed to stimulate, to wake you up. Even small quantities will have an effect on your sleep – the caffeine can remain in your system for six to twelve hours, sometimes longer.

For the sake of an untroubled rest, consider avoiding coffee altogether in the afternoons and evenings.

PRESS ON THE COOL

You can add a degree of sensuality to your rest, and press away the tensions of the day at the same time, with a simple silk eyepress.

Fill a small silk bag with lentils or linseeds, place it over your closed eyes, and feel the gentle relaxation envelop your entire body.

NATURE'S TRANQUILLISER

Valerian is known as nature's tranquilliser. It is a herb that helps to reduce tension in your nervous system.

Whether taken in tablet, tincture or tea, valerian can be effective in transforming restlessness into peaceful rest – without the drowsy hangover effect produced by many chemical sedatives.

LIE BACK AND ENJOY IT

There will be times when sleep is not
meant to happen. On such occasions you
have a choice: either lose sleep over
losing sleep, or appreciate the sheer
luxury of having nothing to do and a
few hours of peace in which to do it.

Treat those moments as an indulgence.
Rest easy in the knowledge that, even if
you're not sleeping, you're still getting
valuable rest.

MEDITATE EARLY

Although meditation will work wonders in helping you to rest better, you may discover that doing it just before you retire can have a rousing effect.

The ideal times for meditation are the times when you want to feel refreshed and awake: early mornings and early evenings. Meditate then and you'll sleep like a baby at night.

SAY CHEESE IN THE SUN

A good level of calcium in the diet
helps to overcome sleeplessness.

Not only will you find calcium in dairy
products such as cheese, but in leafy
green vegetables, almonds, tofu and
some fish. For the calcium to be
effectively metabolised by the body, you
also need vitamin D, which is absorbed
through the skin from sunlight. (Coffee
and alcohol inhibit its effectiveness.)

DREAM OF SLEEP

Whenever you feel that sleep will never
come, conjure a picture of yourself
dreaming. Imagine what you look like in
that state, how you sound, what the bed
feels like beneath you. Chances are,
you'll soon become part of that dream.
Make it a happy one.

PRETEND IT'S THE THIRTIES

Remember the beautiful silk pyjamas the Hollywood movie goddesses used to wear in the thirties? How could you fail to sleep beautifully in pyjamas like those?

Indulge yourself with quality silk worn next to your bare flesh, and your bedtime will take on a pleasurable dimension you may never have considered.

RELISH THE ACT OF CREATION

The moments of your day when you are most creative, are those moments just before you fall asleep.

According to Arthur Koestler, 'The most fertile region [in the mind's inner landscape] seems to be the marshy shore between sleep and full awakening.'

Relax and enjoy it.

SOAK BEFORE SLEEP

A leisurely warm bath before bedtime dissolves all the day's tension from your muscles and gently puts you in the mood for sleep. Surprisingly, this practice is even more relaxing on those occasions you would least expect it — in warm weather. Add a few drops of lavender and marjoram oils, and your rest will be all the more tranquil.

MAKE LOVE

Nothing releases tension, takes your mind off the day-to-day, and prepares you for tomorrow like making love. Have sex with someone you love, and the contented feelings that follow will make your sleep even more satisfying.

THROW OFF A BLANKET

It's hard to imagine sleep without blankets. While the ideal is to be warm, and to be covered, the heavier your covers, the lighter your sleep.

'Just right' normally brings a sounder and more pleasant sleep, than 'warm as toast'.

DROP ON YOUR PILLOW

A couple of drops of marjoram or lavender oils, or your favourite relaxing essential oil, will not only encourage sleep, but pleasant dreams as well.

Drop the oil onto a handkerchief and slip it inside your pillow case.

HAVE A BALL UNDER THE COVERS

Chiropractors say that many, if not most, stiff necks stem from sleeping habits – primarily, from sleeping on the stomach.

A simple way to overcome this habit is to place a tennis ball in the pocket of your pyjamas. The subtle discomfort that arises from this will encourage you to sleep on your side or back.

NO NEWS IS GOOD NEWS

Getting lost in an involving, or even a boring book can be a great way to unwind in the moments before sleep.

Newspapers and news magazines, on the other hand, can have the opposite effect. These publications are invariably filled with gloom and negative reports – not the sort of stuff you want colouring your thoughts and feelings at the end of the day.

SNUGGLE

You can double the cosiness and satisfaction of your sleep simply by snuggling up to a friendly body.

The contentment that flows from this should make you feel like sleeping.

GET IT OFF YOUR CHEST

There is nothing like a clear conscience
to clear the way for an untroubled rest.

INVEST IN MATTRESS REAL ESTATE

You are more intimate with your mattress, and spend much more time with it, than any other piece of furniture.

Invest in your mattress: the bigger and firmer your mattress, the more luxurious your sleep.

WAKE WHEN YOU'RE TOLD TO

You can live without an alarm clock. If you simply tell yourself that, 'Tomorrow I will wake at 7.00 am', you will wake at 7.00 am. As long as you trust your subconscious and don't keep checking the clock throughout the night, you will wake on the dot. Every time.

MULL UP SOME MULBERRY

Take one teaspoonful of this mixture,
twice daily, to help you sleep: boil a
kilogram of fresh mulberries in water.
After 30 minutes, pour out the water
and keep, add more and boil again.
After another 30 minutes add the
original liquid, and reduce. Then add
honey and continue to boil for two
more minutes.

DON'T LOSE SLEEP OVER NOT SLEEPING

One of the peculiarities of being wide awake in bed is that it often induces an anxiety of its own.

If you can view life as an adventure – where you can never accurately predict the outcome – then being awake simply becomes part of that adventure. Who knows where it will lead? Who knows what you will discover about yourself in the tranquil moments of half sleep?

SLEEP WITH A CHAMOMILE

Chamomile is one of nature's gentlest
and most effective relaxants.

It is readily available as a tea which
you can modify to your taste with
honey and lemon. Equally as relaxing,
add a few drops of chamomile oil to
your bath before bedtime.

BECOME A TODDLER

Have you ever noticed how small
children sleep? They drift off as though
they don't have a care in the world, and
their every possible need will be taken
care of.

Dwell on this feeling when you retire
at night: pretend to yourself that you
don't have a care in the world, and that
your every need will be taken care of.
Then you can sleep like a child, too.

WATCH OUT FOR CHINESE

Although this has become less of a problem as we become more aware of dietary issues, the old Chinese flavour enhancer, MSG, is still used in many restaurants.

Monosodium glutamate (MSG) can wreak havoc on your sleep. Avoid it at all costs – if for no other reason than good taste.

SLEEP NATURAL

You may find that synthetic or heavily coloured materials interfere with your body's ability to breathe and your ability to relax properly. Not only does this apply to your daywear, but to your sleepwear as well.

If you want to enjoy the kind of natural slumber that some people will only ever dream about, begin with natural fibres for your bedclothes and bedcovers.

Soothe yourself to sleep

If you are inclined to restlessness
while you are asleep, you will get more
than pleasure out of this sensuous,
pre-bedtime exercise: mix a blend of a
couple of drops each of blue chamomile,
lavender and neroli oils together (in an
almond oil base), and slowly work into
your face, neck and arms, lightly
covering every part of your body until
you are blissfully relaxed.

TRY B3

Many people who suffer from insomnia find that vitamin B3 (niacin) helps bring on sleep. Both vitamins B3 and B6 help convert an amino acid, l-tryptophan, into the hormone that helps you to sleep, serotonin. You'll find both of these vitamins in bananas, corn, brown rice, soybeans, wheatbran, brewer's yeast, peanuts and meats.

KNOW WHEN TO GIVE IN

It's quite natural for all human beings to have disturbed sleep at certain times of the month or at certain ages. When these occasions arise, it's important to recognise that there's little to be gained in struggling for sleep. These are the occasions to give in gracefully, get out of bed and savour the stillness of the night.

TAKE AN AUTHOR TO BED

Most authors would like their novel to be a riveting, thought-provoking experience. Yet, most people find a good story is a great way to relax and unwind. Especially in bed.

There is a physiological reason for this: as you lose yourself in the reading of a book, you progressively ease into a relaxed, trance-like state.

SLEEP ON YOUR FOOD

Overeating and undereating will both
disturb your sleep. Eat too much, and
your metabolism is quickened and the
digestive system has to work harder,
causing you to toss and turn through
the night. Eat too little and hunger
interferes with your rest.

Snack on calming foods such as
oatmeal and wholewheat bread and
you'll sleep better.

SURF

It has long been celebrated that sailors (and surfers and divers) sleep more soundly than landlubbers.

There's a lesson to be learned here: if you want to assure yourself of a blissful, deep sleep, spend time in, on, near, or beneath the waves.

KNIT ONE, PEARL TWO

I sometimes think that knitting was
designed as a productive form of
meditation.

The repetitive nature of the needles and
patterns are hypnotic in their action,
and soon lull you into a deeply relaxed
state. From this state, you can move on
to sleep, or you can wake – the choice
is yours.

LOVE LAVENDER

The lavender flower is one of nature's
most seductive relaxants. In days past,
lavender water was a widely-used scent
and relaxant. Even Keats recognised its
charm in his poem, 'The Eve of
St Agnes':

And still she slept an azure-lidded sleep,
In blanched linen, smooth, and lavendered.

GIVE YOUR FOOT THE KNUCKLE

The sole of the foot is the source of dozens of acupressure points that relate to how relaxed you feel.

To ease yourself into a deeply relaxed state, take your left foot in your left hand and, with the knuckles of your right hand, gently rock backwards and forwards between arch and ball.

GROW OLD GRACEFULLY

As you get older, you may sometimes experience a return to the sleep patterns of early childhood: napping during the day, as well as at night.

While this may mean you require less sleep at night, it is entirely natural – something neither to resist, nor be alarmed about.

EXPLORE THE SUBTLETIES
OF FOREIGN CINEMA

One of the unsung attractions of the
more 'subtle' foreign films is their
ability to start you yawning. Such
films, or indeed any cultural activity
that affects you this way, may have
much to offer in your search for a way
of producing sleep.

FANTASISE

When you go to bed tonight, treat
yourself to a fantasy.

Make believe you're lying on a sun-
bleached tropical island. You can see a
solitary cloud floating through the sky
above, and hear the quiet lapping of
waves on the shore. You can feel the
sand beneath your back and the warmth
of the sun on your face. Fantasise that
you're drifting off, drifting off . . .

TRY SLEEPING WITH ROSE

If you believe in the soothing and
healing power of crystals, sleep with
a Rose Quartz 'Love Stone' under
your pillow.

Scientists agree that crystals such as
Rose Quartz do have unique physical
properties; believers agree that they
have the power to remove pressure and
relax the mind.

SLEEP QUIETLY,

*now that
the gates of the day
are closed. Leave tomorrow's
problems for tomorrow.*

*The earth is peaceful.
Only the stars are abroad;
and they will not
cause you any trouble.*

'SLEEP', MAX EHRMANN

HAVE CHOCOLATE FOR BREAKFAST

For some, life would be unbearable without chocolate. Others feel the same about cola.

If you must have stimulants such as chocolate, cola or coffee, have them before lunch. Even smaller amounts later in the day can produce restlessness at night.

TAKE THE PASSION TO BED

The exotic sounding passion flower or passifiora has been used as a sedative for centuries. It works as a calming agent on the nervous system.

You will find passion flower, along with other relaxing herbs – such as hops, lemon balm and limeflower – in teas in your health food store.

CHILL YOUR PILLOW

There is nothing more relaxing and conducive towards rest than a cool, cotton pillow case on a warm summer evening.

On really warm nights, try leaving your pillow case in the refrigerator for a few minutes before retiring. It will help lower your body temperature, which helps bring on sleep.

BREAKFAST AT NIGHT

More than most other foodstuffs,
humble oats are known for their
calming as well as their nutritional
properties.

A plate of porridge with milk,
therefore, can be the ideal pre-bedtime
snack. (You might have difficulty
explaining it to your house
guests, though.)

GIVE OR TAKE AN HOUR

Some people feel cheated if they miss an hour or two of sleep at night.

However, studies show that six or seven hours of sound sleep will leave you feeling significantly more rested in the morning than eight or nine hours of tossing and turning.

With sleep, quality outweighs quantity every time. So don't feel short-changed if you miss an hour or two.

SHRUG OFF LONELINESS

The stillness of the night exaggerates loneliness.

The antidote to loneliness is to become comfortable with, and to enjoy the pleasure of, your own company. This may seem like an effort but, once you have mastered this subtle shift of attitude, you may discover what good company you can be.

Turn to your brain

One of the functions of the brain is to produce melatonin, a neurochemical that helps to lower your body temperature and induce sleepiness.

In many countries, melatonin can now be bought without prescription as an aid to sleep and as an aid to moderate jet lag. But, as with all artificial sleep-inducers, even so-called natural ones, professional advice should be sought.

LET DAWN SEND YOU TO SLEEP

How many poor sleepers do you know who are early risers? Not many.

While you may discover something refreshing and invigorating about being up before the sun rises, the real appeal of early rising is that it encourages sleep at the end of the day — and that makes rising early *tomorrow* morning even more appealing.

SHIFT FORWARDS

When your job involves shift work, the
best way of maintaining a degree of
harmony and comfort in your sleep
patterns is to follow the clock
forwards.

Next time you change your shift hours,
change them in a forward direction,
rather than backwards. Do this and
your sleep patterns will adjust more
harmoniously.

THE GOOD OIL ON SLEEP

'Alternative' people have long believed
that essential oils such as lavender,
marjoram and neroli possess calming
properties. Now scientific evidence
proves this is so: the aromas of these
oils aid the production of serotonin, the
chemical that helps you to sleep.

Use them in a massage base or a
ceramic burner, and discover just how
relaxing they can be.

PRETEND YOU'RE SPANISH

There is a belief that the siesta relates more to late lunches and warm weather than to rest cycles. However the human rest cycle does occur twice a day and the other time is in the early afternoon.

If you find that a 'normal' night-time sleep cycle eludes you, consider this sensible Latin habit.

RISE AT SIX FORTY-FIVE

Regardless of what hour you get to bed
at night, make a practice of waking at
the same time every day. The more
habitual your rising time becomes, the
more habitual your falling asleep
time becomes.

MAKE REST A RITUAL

Similarly, the more ritualised your
bedtime, the more patterns you
establish, the more you condition
yourself to falling asleep at a specific
time in the evening. Make a routine of
bedtime, and you make a routine
of sleep.

CATNAP ON OCCASIONS

There will be times when sleep escapes you. You have a choice: either rail against wakefulness or accept what has been dealt, and make up for it tomorrow.

If you choose the latter, you can get by with brief catnaps during the day. As long as you accept that this may be disruptive to your night-time rest, it can make your days more bearable.

AVOID CATNAPS AT ALL COST

If you want to make a routine of restful sleep, sleep only at night.

That means avoiding catnaps during the day at all cost — regardless of how much sleep you have lost the previous evening. Catnaps during the day will often extract a price from your sleep at night. The choice is yours.

The best cure for insomnia is to get
lots of sleep.

W. C. FIELDS

SINK AND SLEEP

An entertaining way of forgetting about sleeplessness is to concentrate on all the external sensations of your body.

Feel the air on your face, your head on the pillow. Feel your skin against the bedclothes. When you can feel the entire length of your body slowly sinking into the mattress, you will be well on the way to sinking into oblivion.

BECOME WELL READ

Some of the best-read people I've met have difficulty sleeping at night. They have time to indulge their passion.

At the risk of appearing defeatist, if you do have to endure periods of sleeplessness, celebrate the fact that you've found the solution to one of life's most common complaints: 'I don't have the time.'

Use that time to become well read.

TAKE FRENCH LESSONS

Several of the French composers from
the late Romantic and early
Impressionist eras made an art of
relaxing, entrancing music. Indulge
yourself with the compositions of
Debussy, Fauré, Bizet and Satie – not
only to ease into a relaxed state, but to
fill your night and soul with beauty.

REST BY THE SEA

Ever noticed how soundly you sleep
when you're within earshot of the surf?
There is more to this than the freshness
of sea air: the rhythm of the ebb and
flow of waves is almost identical to the
breathing of a deeply relaxed person.

Even if you don't live by the sea, you
can enjoy the same calming effect by
listening to a recording of ocean waves.

POSTPONE YOUR WORRIES

The worst part about worries is the way they visit in the quiet of the night.

With a minimum of effort you can postpone them until your waking hours – invariably, they will seem less threatening then. Write them down, assuring yourself that you will grant them your full attention the following day.

GO TO SLEEP IN FASHION

As much as bright colours and wispy curtains may please your decorating aesthetics, they are not always conducive to sound sleep. Dark bedrooms, or at the very minimum, light-proof curtains, are your starting point for an uninterrupted rest.

HIDE THE CLOCK

The addition of a clock to your
bedroom can be a constant reminder of
any sleep you may be missing out on.
Its very presence is often all that's
necessary to keep your mind ticking
over when it should be at rest.

Leave your clock outside, and you have
a better chance of finding sleep inside.

THINK AHEAD

Small problems become giant ones, and
rational people become irrational when
they're denied sleep. A good way to
reduce the size of problems is to use
your imagination: imagine yourself, in
ten years' time. Try to imagine how
you will feel then about the problems
you're wrestling with now.

Nine times out of ten they'll diminish.

SPRING CLEAN

If all else fails, get out of bed and start
doing something menial and boring –
like spring cleaning, or filing. Be
meticulous and keep going until you
have completed the chore.

Two or three nights is all it takes to
cure the most persistent insomnia.
Sleep comes quickly when you know
the alternative is sitting up polishing
the silver.

KEEP A JOURNAL

Journal writing has much to offer those
who have trouble sleeping. It helps you
to put problems into perspective. It is a
record of your sleep habits. And, over
and above all else, it is a quiet,
reflective activity that often induces a
languor of its own.

HAVE A THREE-HOUR FAMINE

If you want to sleep easily and soundly,
the time to complete dinner is three
hours before bedtime. Providing you
don't go to bed feeling hungry, the
earlier you eat, the better you sleep.

ESCAPE THE LIGHT

Any form of light can inhibit the
production of the protein you require to
produce melatonin, the body's most
important sleep-producing hormone.
Remove all lights from your bedroom,
even the LED glow on your alarm
clock, and you'll sleep better.

BE AWARE OF SIX THINGS

Focus on one bright spot then, with
your peripheral vision, note six
different things you can see. Without
allowing your eyes to stray, note six
different sounds you can hear. Then six
things you can feel. Next, note only
five. Then four, three, two, one . . .

If you're ever going to fall asleep, you
will be asleep by one.

RUB ALONE

There is an effective alternative to receiving a full-body massage which, as we know, coaxes you to the very edge of sleep. The alternative is a sensuous, do-it-yourself massage.

Using a scented massage oil, work each limb – slowly, lazily and in detail – before moving onto the next part of your body. After thirty minutes of this you will be ready for sleep.

LOOK FORWARD TO THE DREAM TIME

When you cease to dream you cease to live.

MALCOLM S. FORBES

Switch off the EMFs

Electromagnetic fields (EMFs) created by electric current or appliances may influence your dominant brain wave states – particularly those you depend on for a good night's sleep.

Banishing electronic influences such as the clock radio or television from your bedroom often banishes one of the great obstacles to sleep.

THE GOOD OIL ON JET LAG

A pleasant way around jet lag is by using essential oils. When you arrive at your destination immediately make yourself a warm bath with a few drops of rosemary and sandalwood oils. After a leisurely soak, go about your business for the day.

TURN OFF THE POWER

A falling body temperature is the
body's way of helping you to fall
asleep. Hence, as appealing as it may
seem on a chilly night, an electric
blanket can interfere with your rest if
left turned on.

For the most luxurious repose, use
your electric blanket to warm the bed
before bedtime – then turn it off before
you retire.

SLEEP ON A SHEEP

As any baby will tell you, a sheepskin underblanket really stands out from the flock when it comes to encouraging the deepest sleep.

This is not just because of the physical sensation. There is a unique property of wool that allows your body to perspire in vapour form rather than liquid, and this contributes to a more relaxed, natural-feeling sleep.

LEARN TO HOVER

Astral travel is not for everybody. But believers and participants insist it always happens in the deepest of sleeps.

You can emulate this experience by imagining your body floating a fraction of a centimetre above the bed. When you can really sense what this feels like you will have put aside all thoughts of the 'here and now' and who knows where you might be headed.

WAIT FOR THE WEARIES

All people are different: most get tired
around ten, some earlier. Others are
still not tired at midnight.

You can make a habit of turning
tiredness into sleep simply by waiting
until you're drowsy before going to
bed. Alternatively, go to bed the
moment you feel drowsy.

STUDY YOUR PILLOW

One pillow could be all that stands between you and a beautiful sleep.

With so many different pillow types on offer today, you can almost certainly find the one that suits your anatomy and temperament. Experiment. You'll probably end up wondering why you've never thought of this before.

CONVINCE YOURSELF
YOU'VE BEEN SLEEPING

Take comfort in the fact that studies
show many people who claim to be
insomniac are either normal sleepers,
or lose less than thirty minutes of sleep
a night. Moreover, most are asleep
within twenty minutes of placing their
head on the pillow.

Often the belief you're not getting
enough sleep is no more than that:
a belief.

LEAVE WORK FOR WORK

Hard-working people often have sleep problems because they don't know how to stop working after going to bed.

Make a ritual of stopping work at a specific time each day. Choose a cut off place, time or event that signals the end of your working day. Make a list of things that should be resumed the following day, then retire for the night with a clear mind.

LIGHT UP YOUR FINGERS

While you lie in bed, imagine a
lightness in the tips of your fingers.
Keep your hands still, and imagine this
lightness almost lifting your fingers
from the bed. Now imagine the same
lightness in your toes. Feel them lifting
upwards. If ten minutes of this doesn't
send you to sleep, it will certainly have
you feeling deeply relaxed, and you
know where that leads . . .

PLUG IN THE QUIET

There is a simple, cheap antidote to noisy neighbours or neighbourhoods: soft ear plugs.

A pleasing alternative is to play soft, relaxing music through headphones. And, if you use the same music each time you do this, you begin to create a calming association with that particular piece – then you'll find it works all the more quickly.

DESIGN AN ANGST STRETCH

Anger can be a major cause of sleep interruption. It is not always easy to forgive or forget.

A more creative alternative is to choose one time and place each day to vent your negative feelings. Do it on your daily walk, for example, on a designated 'angst stretch' – where you exercise your hostile feelings, then abandon them until next time.

ESCAPE OUTDOORS

You will have noticed how tired you feel after spending time in the clean mountain air, or the refreshing sea breeze, or in the wide open spaces. Outdoor places such as these not only help you to feel that you've spent the day well, but also help you to sleep more soundly at night.

Spend time outdoors for a better sleep indoors.

RECALL YOUR LAST FACIAL

Remember how peaceful you felt, how you drifted off into a halcyon state, the last time you had a facial?

You can clone that experience in bed tonight, bring back that deep sense of relaxation, simply by applying a warm, wet face-towel, scented with a few drops of lavender oil.

TURN ON THE HUM

Travellers on submarines and ocean cruisers soon make an amazing discovery about the nature of sound: you sleep soundly while engines are running only to wake when they stop.

The low-pitched hum produced by engines and some air-conditioners often occur at the same frequency that the brain produces, and locks into, in delta sleep.

INSTRUCT YOURSELF TO SLEEP

Often when you have difficulty sleeping, the words that play through your thoughts exacerbate the condition. Unspoken instructions like, 'I'll never get to sleep if this continues,' tend to become self-fulfilling.

Better to issue new (unspoken) instructions for your thoughts, like, 'If I lie here and relax, and listen to my breathing, sleep will soon be here.'

LIGHT UP AND STAY UP

This probably won't make it easier for you to give up smoking, but it is worth recognising that nicotine is a stimulant. A stimulant that disturbs sleep.

If you are committed to being a smoker, yet you want to sleep soundly, avoid cigarettes for at least two hours before bedtime.

St John's Wort

Women who suffer from PMS know how disruptive this can be to their sleep patterns.

While the ubiquitous evening primrose oil does assist, there is another remedy that many believe is even more powerful: St John's wort (hypericum). Its calming and sedative properties help induce sleep without producing drowsiness the following day.

PRAY FOR SLEEP

There is a psychological benefit from
prayer that is often overlooked in the
spirituality that accompanies it. Within
the brain is a place sometimes referred
to as 'the God spot'. Accessing this
place mentally will produce feelings of
peace and transcendence.

Those who pray, and derive comfort and
satisfaction from the activity, are
seldom left feeling sleep-deprived.

DOWN THE WILD JUJUBE

There is a range of herbs in Chinese medicine used to treat sleep problems – wild jujube, lotus seed and many more.

You might never have these prescribed, however, because traditional Chinese herbalists eschew simplistic diagnoses such as 'insomnia', and may search for more relevant underlying conditions.

If you have a chronic sleep disorder, Chinese herbalism could work for you.

GET FRESH WITH YOUR SHEETS

What is it about crisp, fresh linen that makes you want to drift off the moment you slip between the covers?

Whether it's the simple, physical sensation of that freshly laundered surface, or the thought of approaching the night untainted by the past, it is an experience that's worth exploring on a regular basis. Use fresh sheets as often as your laundry will allow.

CHOOSE BETWEEN SLEEP AND VAMPIRES

For hundreds of years, garlic has been one of the favoured safeguards against vampire attack at night. Perhaps the way it works is in preventing you from sleeping too deeply.

As some yogis will tell you, excessive garlic, salt and spices induce restlessness. Too much late at night is a recipe for unrest.

ADD SOME ADVENTURE

Some people have disrupted sleep at night because they haven't exhausted enough mental and physical energy throughout the day.

Use your body and your brain during the day. Look out for little adventures. Take on a few physical and mental challenges. Then you can rest easy at night.

GET OUT OF THE HOUSE

Melatonin is the hormone that makes your body want to sleep. Sunlight (which produces melanin) encourages the body to readily produce this hormone.

If illness or disability confines you to the house, try to submit yourself to a little sunshine as often as you can. It may help you to sleep better.

TURN THE ROOM BLUE

Colours, like sounds, not only have an impact on your emotions, but on your physiology as well. The wavelengths of colours such as blue and green, or pastel pink, encourage restful feelings – whereas the more dynamic primary colours stimulate.

Paint your bedroom with restful colours and you'll find rest comes much easier.

START AT THE TEMPLE

One of the most relaxing acupressure points on the body is one you intuitively reach for when you're under pressure – at your temples.

Massage your temples in a light circular motion, then stroke your forehead from your eyebrows past the temples, and you'll stroke yourself into a deeper and deeper state of relaxation.

EXPECT NOTHING

One of the most comforting pieces of
advice ever offered by an old Zen
master was this: expect nothing.
Sometimes sleep is good, sometimes it
is merely okay, sometimes you miss out
altogether. This is the way of life.
Expect nothing, and you'll enjoy
whatever arrives all the more.

TAKE TO THE TANK

While you may not hear a lot about them these days, float tanks can work wonders in de-stressing the body and, subsequently, enriching your sleep.

Float in the late afternoon and you'll sleep all the sounder at night.

If there's no float tank nearby, you can create your own with low lights, bath salts and warm water – in the privacy and familiarity of your own bathroom.

PRACTISE SOLITAIRE

The card game, solitaire, was designed
to send you to sleep.

Undemanding, repetitive, requiring
concentration but little mental effort, it
will soon lull you into a numbed state.
If you can resist the urge to believe
your next hand will be the complete
one, you will find this pastime both
relaxing and tiring.

STOP

Any activity that you find intellectually or emotionally stimulating — be it listening to music, stamp collecting, or reading a novel — has the capacity to interfere with your sleep . . . if participated in last thing before retiring.

Abandon these activities at least an hour before you retire, and your rest will come easier.

BREATHE SLEEPILY

Have you ever noticed how relaxed a
sleeping person's breathing sounds?
Slow, deep, measured. You can use
these same techniques to ease yourself
into a relaxed, drowsy state.

Simply breathe deeply, concentrating on
the bottom of your lungs rather than
your chest; gradually slow down your
breathing until the breaths become more
and more leisurely.

ENJOY THE SILENCE

We live in an age when silence is often considered a vacuum to be filled, or as an absence rather than a gain.

The wonder of silence is that it is the first step towards becoming calm and at peace – something to be pursued and appreciated, rather than avoided.

Regard silence this way, seek it in the evening before bedtime, and you will rest easier as the evening grows still.

HEAL IN THE MORNING

Many medications, both pharmaceutical and herbal, can stimulate certain responses that interfere with your sleep. This can also apply to some vitamin supplements.

To remove this obstacle to your slumber, if possible take such medications in the morning or during the day.

SEEK VARIETY OUT OF BED

Although different people need different amounts of sleep, those who follow the most disciplined sleeping routine usually claim to have the most satisfactory sleep. The same number of hours each night, every night, without variation.

If you feel your life needs variety, seek that variety in your waking hours — not in your sleeping hours.

SPEND YOURSELF

Physical exhaustion is a sure course to sound sleep. Whether your exhaustion comes from intense exercise, dance, love-making or a hard day at work, the results are the same – deep, satisfying sleep.

The converse of this is also true: while inactivity, sloth and boredom may still produce tiredness, they will not lead to a satisfying rest.

ROLL OVER

The most relaxed sleeping position is not on your stomach, and probably not even on your side: it's on your back.

Providing you're not one to snore, sleep on your back and your body will rest more efficiently.

Sleep on your back and your breathing will be deeper.

Sleep on your back.

WAXING DREAMILY ABOUT WAX

Far out! Something sleep-inducing, but still legal, did come out of the sixties.

The lava lamp.

While some may question its role in decor aesthetics, the entrancing, changing shapes of its rising and falling molten wax can have you nodding off in no time.

WRITE OUT OF WORRIES

Even small worries have the capacity to hamper your sleep. One of the most efficient worry eliminators, or at least normalisers, is the notebook.

If you find yourself with worries or problems before bedtime, jot them down in a notebook – then analyse the likelihood of their eventuating, work them through, or postpone them until a specific time tomorrow.

PUT BEADS IN YOUR BED

Over the centuries, worry beads, prayer beads and prayer wheels have been used by millions of devoted owners to dispense with nervous tension and to discover calm states.

Some say it's the repetitive action of the fingering, others say it's the stimulation of relaxing acupressure points in the hands. Either way, it is a simple, tangible way to drowsiness.

CRADLE YOUR FINGER

There are many well-rested people who swear by the following getting-to-sleep ritual: lightly grasp the forefinger of one hand in the palm of the other, and cradle it until you doze off.

This is an eastern energy-balancing technique that capitalises on the reflexology meridians in the hand in order to help you relax.

FEEL YOUR TUMMY

When you breathe really deeply, your
lower abdomen – not your chest and
shoulders – swells with each breath.

If you can feel your tummy rise and fall
this way, you're only a few breaths
away from being deeply relaxed.
Concentrate on breathing deeply, then
breathing slowly, and you'll soon be
ready to doze. (If not, you'll still enjoy
a state of deep relaxation.)

LIGHT UP A JOSS STICK

There is a property in smouldering incense that stimulates the production of serotonin, the neurochemical that helps you get to sleep.

While it may not be a good idea to burn anything in the bedroom itself, incense can have a powerfully relaxing effect in the hours leading to bedtime.

RESET THE CLOCK

Just half an hour's exposure to the morning sunlight is usually all it takes to reset your body clock after a long flight, nursing a new baby throughout the night, or any period of interrupted sleep.

Expose yourself to the sun in the morning, and you'll find it easier to sleep after the sun has set.

PRETEND TO BE INNOCENT

Deservedly, the innocent enjoy a soundness of sleep that the rest of us only fantasise about.

As you lie in bed, think back on a time of your own innocence – when your life was ruled by optimism and wonder, untempered by deadlines and responsibilities – and let your imagination re-experience those restful feelings tonight.

INDULGE YOUR BODY

There are few experiences in life that can relax, and put you in the mood for sleep, as effectively as a full-body massage. The effects are equally as powerful be it Swedish, Shiatsu, Hawaiian or Korean.

Treat yourself as often as you can afford. Justify it on the basis that it is as good for the sleep as it is for the soul.

FORMULA FOR A BEAUTIFUL SLEEP

A guaranteed formula for a beautiful sleep: sleep in a beautiful bed, sleep under beautiful bedclothes, wear beautiful nightwear, and delight in it all under beautiful soft bedroom lights.

TRY A DIFFERENT RHYTHM

The circadian rhythm for many people is not a strict 24 hours. If we were to live in a place with no clocks or sunlight (as experienced by underground cavers), some would sleep an hour longer each day.

You can use this to vary your own rhythm: go to bed one hour later every night for a week. You should be ready to fall asleep one hour earlier of an evening after this.

FORGET NORMS

Please remember: if you have erratic sleep patterns, what you are experiencing is probably entirely normal. At any given time, a huge proportion of the population is sharing that same experience.

The good news is that, in most cases, it's temporary. And regular, restful sleep will come again.

TAKE A BREAK BY YOURSELF

If you live in a crowded or noisy
household, you could profit by
following this pre-bedroom ritual: go
to another room and devote half an hour
to yourself, alone with your thoughts,
without stimulation of any kind.

Take pleasure in your own company for
this time, and be surprised how readily
sleep follows.

TRIM DOWN

Excess body fat and restlessness often go hand in hand. As one of the first areas the body stores fat is at the base of the tongue, snoring and sleep apnoea frequently accompany obesity.

Generally, the moment you begin to lose weight, you start to sleep better – some would find that a double incentive to watch their diet.

TRAIN YOUR BED

You can train yourself to associate your bed with restfulness rather than wakefulness by the practices you adopt.

Sleep-inducing beds permit only two activities: sleeping and sex. All other activities should be banished to other places – preferably other rooms.

GET THE BRUSH OUT

You can extract a dual benefit from brushing your hair, or having it brushed, before bedtime.

For a start, the gentle, repetitive action is calming in its own right. More importantly, brushing stimulates many of the relaxing acupressure points in the scalp, which gives you a real head start on getting to sleep.

O SLEEP

O gentle sleep,
Nature's soft nurse! how have I
frighted thee,
That thou no more wilt weigh my
eyelids down
And steep my senses in forgetfulness?

HENRY IV, WILLIAM SHAKESPEARE

CLEAR THE AIR

As houses can be traps for household dust, dust mites, animal hair and other pollutants, an air purifier, or even an ioniser, can clear the way to a better sleep.

Keep your bedroom pollutant-free, especially by denying your pets access. Before you know it, you'll be sleeping like a kitten.

THINK ABOUT YAWNS

You've been conditioning yourself since childhood to associate yawning with sleep.

Ever noticed how you start yawning the moment someone else does? The same thing happens if you can imagine someone yawning: the clearer you can visualise this action, the more catching it becomes, and you start yawning yourself.

TURN AWAY FROM THE TUBE

While a book can be an ideal way to ease yourself into sleep mode, television often has the opposite effect. It is surprising how often you find the program that was sending you to sleep while you were watching it, will suddenly stimulate your thoughts the moment you go to bed.

BEWARE OF THE FIZZ

You know colas are laced with caffeine.
But did you know that other, seemingly
benign soft drinks also have a caffeine
content? Some do. If you want to avoid
restlessness, avoid fizzy drinks
at night.

Jet Into Bed

When you fly from one time zone to
another, and jet lag becomes a risk,
there is a simple procedure that will
help you quickly adjust on arrival.
Sleep for an hour or two after you land,
then remain active until night. Next
morning, you can adjust your body
clock by allowing sunlight onto your
skin at the first opportunity.

REVISIT A FABULOUS MOMENT

Add pleasure and beauty to those moments before sleep by reliving a beautiful experience.

Devote your full attention to it as you lie in bed. Visualise every detail, recall every sound, and try to recapture the feelings.

What a fabulous way to drift off.

TALK UP A DREAM

The words you use have a distinct effect on the thoughts and attitudes you have. This can be the difference between feeling positive or negative.

Talk yourself into tiredness by choosing words that relate to this sensation.

Try these instead: 'I am feeling a great sense of peace and relief as I let go of the problems of the day, and gradually ease into a carefree, blissful sleep.'

LOOK UP TO THE CLOUDS

Biofeedback experiments reveal that the simple act of looking upwards, with unfocused eyes, induces a restful state.

Make it even more restful by visualising a moving restful image. Imagine a small fluffy cloud floating through a clear blue sky. Imagine another following it. And another.

In a way, it's like counting sheep. Except it works.

PLAY THE SATURDAY GAME

Notice how much easier it is to sleep
on Friday or Saturday nights? There's
no work tomorrow and it doesn't matter
if you oversleep in the morning.

Pretend it's Saturday tonight.
Close your eyes and imagine waking up
to a perfect day tomorrow. The sun will
be shining and you will rise to find the
last day of a restful weekend still ahead
of you.

BATHE AT THE END OF THE BED

A splendid little luxury almost totally overlooked in today's fast world is the footbath. Warm water, three or four drops of your favourite calming oil, a few rose petals, a fluffy white towel, and twenty minutes of bliss.

Do this at the end of your bed so that you'll be ready for sleep before the sense of indulgence has passed.

AVOID PUBERTY

The onset of puberty is usually accompanied by a reduction in the secretion of melatonin, the hormone that regulates your biorhythms and helps make you sleepy. Bear this in mind next time puberty approaches.

TURN THE OTHER WAY

Sometimes changing the lie of your bed can overcome persistent sleeplessness.

The nature of the Chinese art of *feng shui* is to align your living area with certain natural forces. This means your bed must never face the door, or be under an exposed beam. And mirrors, and furniture with sharp edges, must never face the bed.

What do you have to lose?

HOWL AT THE MOON

If you toss and turn on the night of a full moon, relax – millions of others are tossing and turning in exactly the same way.

TAKE CARE WITH CHEMICALS

While prescription sedatives may sometimes be useful, they should be treated with caution. If you must use them, be aware that many pharmaceutical sedatives will deny you a full REM sleep, and may cause disrupted sleep patterns for some time after you've stopped using them.

PASS THE SUGAR

A common cause of waking during the night is low blood sugar levels. You can easily prevent this happening by having a light snack before you retire.

SLEEP LIKE A BABY

When you have a new baby in the house, sleep deprivation becomes a matter of course.

To add a semblance of regular sleep to your schedule, learn to sleep when baby sleeps (up to eighteen hours a day).

While those brief snatches may feel unsatisfying, in the long run they will help you feel more rested.

THINK OF CAESAR

In Julius Caesar's time, the popular
treatment for insomnia was an infusion
made from the flower of the bitter
orange tree. Today, this same ingredient
is readily available in the form of the
essential oil neroli.

Add a few drops to your bath water.
Sprinkle a drop on your pillow case.
And doze off with pleasant memories of
a distant age.

TAKE CARE OF YOUR DAY

The attitudes and activities that make
up your day invariably impact on the
way you sleep at night. Concentrate on
making your day as fulfilling and
harmonious as possible, perform every
daytime action to the best of your
ability, and you'll find it easier to
enjoy trouble-free sleep at night.

POINT AT YOUR WRIST

There is a powerful relaxing
acupressure point at the crease of your
wrist directly up from your ring finger —
you will feel a small, sensitive
indentation at this place.

By applying a firm downward pressure
with your forefinger as you breathe
out, then releasing the pressure as you
breathe in, you will ease yourself into
a calmer and calmer state.

TAKE YOUR TIME

You'll feel better about your sleeping
routine just by applying a little
patience.

Long-term sleep problems are not
always solved overnight. Take your
time finding a solution. Strive for little
improvements. As long as the
improvement trend line is positive,
you're heading in the right direction.

GET READY FOR BED
BEFORE SUNSET

The moment your head hits the pillow
is not the time to start shedding your
thoughts of the day, and making your
preparations for tomorrow.

Better to start preparing for sleep
earlier in the afternoon, either working
through the issues of the day or
postponing them.

GIVE UP YOUR DIET

How long have you been searching for
the perfect excuse to abandon that
radical diet?

Here it is: strict dieting often has an
adverse effect on the quality of your
sleep. A sensible, well-balanced diet is
the first step to a sensible,
well-balanced sleep.

FILL YOUR MIND WITH NOTHING

One of the hindrances to a sound sleep is the restlessness of thought. By its very nature, thought is restless, constantly moving from one concept to another.

Thoughts can be quelled simply by filling the mind with something else. Concentrate on the sound of your breathing. Or, begin a mantra meditation.

POKE YOUR TONGUE

Stress has a habit of encouraging two conditions, often interlinked: disturbed sleep and tightened jaw muscles. When your jaw muscles are clenched and you grind your teeth, tension begins to spread to other parts of your body.

You can overcome this by lightly pressing your tongue against the roof of your mouth.

CHOOSE YOUR BED
PARTNERS WELL

Don't tell the person beside you that I said this, but one of the most common causes of sleep disturbance is not your attitude or physiology.

It is your partner.

If you sleep with someone who is noisy or restless, consider one of the following: get twin beds, wear earplugs or, in extreme cases, have separate rooms.

BREATHE YOURSELF AWAKE

How do you stay awake the day after a sleepless night? Many think coffee is the answer, but it can disrupt the *next* night's sleep.

A better way is to use a yoga technique known as circular breathing. Cover one nostril, breathe in. Cover the other nostril, breathe out. Breathe in through the same nostril. Cover the other one and breathe out. Continue until you are wide awake.

REMEMBER GRANDMA

Remember what your grandmother used to say about retiring early? 'An hour's sleep before midnight is worth two after.'

Who am I to argue with Grandma?

ABOUT THE AUTHOR

Paul Wilson is known the world over as the 'guru of calm'.

His first book, *The Calm Technique*, is considered one of the most influential in the genre. His second, *Instant Calm*, was a giant bestseller translated into eighteen languages. The success continued with *Calm at Work*, *The Little Book of Calm at Work* and *The Little Book of Pleasure*.

However, the book that won the greatest acclaim is *The Little Book of Calm*. With sales of over 3,000,000 it has spent more than 2 years at the top of the bestseller lists.

Now, with *The Little Book of Sleep*, the peace begins to spread in a slightly new direction.

Feel free to contact the author or share your calm at
http://www.calmcentre.com